With Faith

Accompanying Workbook

Tamara Anderson

This book is formatted and intended to be a companion to With Faith © 2016.

Copyright © 2016 by Tamara Anderson Books

All rights reserved. No part of this publication may be reproduced, distributed, or transmitted in any form or by any means, including photocopying, recording, or other electronic or mechanical methods, without the prior written permission of the publisher, except in the case of brief quotations embodied in critical reviews and certain other noncommercial uses permitted by copyright law.

Printed in the United States of America

First Edition, 2016

ISBN 978-09972879-2-9

Tamara Anderson Books
PO Box 1032
O'Fallon, IL 62269

www.TamaraAndersonBooks.net

Book formatted and edited by Tracy Isley in St. Louis, MO. Cover design by Larry Leonard © 2016. Scripture quotations are from the New King James Version. Copyright © 1982 by Thomas Nelson. Used by permission. All rights reserved.

Preface

This workbook is intended to be a study companion with the book **With Faith**. The workbook chapters go hand-in-hand with the book chapters. There are two types of questions: fill- in-the-blank and short-answer. The fill-in-the-blank questions come from sentences within their respective chapters in **With Faith**. These answers have a correct word(s) to complete the sentence. The short-answer questions are designed to be thought provoking and have no right or wrong answer. The whole purpose of the workbook is to cause you to dig deep within and to grow your faith to the next level.

Table of Contents

Chapter

1	**My Faith**	1
2	**What is Faith**	6
3	**Fruit of Faith**	11
4	**Gift of Faith**	16
5	**Faith is More Than Believing**	21
6	**Faith Through Testimonies**	24
7	**Jeri's Testimony**	28
8	**Dangerous D's**	32
9	**Doubt**	37
10	**Unbelief**	42
11	**My Fears**	46
12	**Fear by satan**	50
13	**Fear of the Lord**	54
14	**With Faith**	57
15	**Tiffany's Testimony**	61
	Book Summation	65

Chapter 1

MY FAITH

Questions for You to Consider

I went through an experience that tested my faith. What situation have you encountered that has tested your faith?

_____

_____

_____

_____

My faith dwindled during my test. Did your faith diminish while you were being tested?

_____

_____

_____

_____

Upon hearing the news of my miscarriage, I immediately knew that I had fallen short during my faith test. What was your "ah hah" moment that let you know you missed the mark on your faith test?

_____

_____

_____

_____

_____

The enemy had me hosting a pity party and feeling trapped in condemnation. How did you feel and what did you face after your test?

_____

_____

_____

_____

_____

One day I heard the voice of the Lord say "you have been here long enough. It is time to get up, dust yourself off, learn this lesson, and get to moving! It is time for you to be about your Father's business." What occurred that enabled you to "dust yourself off" and continue your walk in Christ?

_____

_____

_____

_____

_____

I was able to learn this lesson of faith and stand against the devil as other test came upon me. Where you able to learn the lesson of faith after this test? If not, what did you do differently during your next test?

_____

_____

_____

_____

Chapter Summation

After taking a deeper look into your test(s) of faith, what have you learned about yourself? About faith?

_____

_____

_____

_____

Life Application

What do you plan to do differently going forward?

Chapter 1 Review

- We are all going to have to face faith tests.
- You may not pass every one of them.

- If you miss the mark - pick yourself up, dust yourself off, and continue on your Christian walk.
- If you pass with flying colors, congrats and remember the tools that enabled you to pass to ensure that you pass the next test.

Chapter 2

WHAT IS FAITH?

Questions for You to Consider

In your own words, what is faith?

_____

_____

_____

_____

_____

Faith According to the World

_____ _____ _____ is based on faith. We have _____ in our _____ lives and don't even realize it.

Put a check mark (■) next to the entities you have put your faith in:

_____ Bank   _____ Credit Card Company

_____ Car   _____ Job

_____ Chair   _____ Money

Other than the examples given in the book, can you think of instances where faith is used in our everyday lives?

_____

_____

_____

_____

_____

Faith According to the Word

Write out Hebrews 11:1 in which ever translation you desire. As you write it, speak it out loud.

_____

_____

_____

_____

When, where and what was the last testimony you heard that glorified our Savior?

_____

_____

_____

_____

Faith can only be received as a _____ from God and it's something that can never be _____ in and of ourselves.

Can you think of the last time someone has not kept their word/promise? Explain the situation.

_____

_____

_____

_____

_____

Think of the last promise you received from God. Did you wait for it like Abraham or did you take matters into your own hands like Sarah?

_____

_____

_____

_____

_____

Chapter Summation

After taking a contrasting look at faith according to the world and faith according to the word, what have you learned?

Life Application

What do you plan to do differently going forward?

Chapter 2 Review

- Faith can have many different definitions or synonyms to many different people.
- Our whole life is based on faith. We have faith in our everyday lives and don't even realize it.
- Faith according to the world is *un*like faith according to the word.
    - In the world, faith is put into banks, credit card companies, jobs and money.
    - Faith placed into these entities will fail you.
- Faith according to the word is best described in *Hebrews 11:1 AMP, Now faith is the assurance (the confirmation, the title deed) of the things [we] hope for, being the proof of things [we] do not see and the conviction of their reality [faith perceiving as real fact what is not revealed to the senses].*
- Faith is a gift from God and it's something that can never be established in and of ourselves.
- Faith is God's warranty for us which guarantees the fulfillment of His promises to the believers. God's warranty is not man's warranty.
- Faith is God's divine persuasion or marvelous influence in our lives. We have to be fully persuaded that He will do what He has promised and we have to know that these promises will come to pass His way.

Chapter 3

FRUIT OF FAITH

Questions for You to Consider

Everyone who is filled with the precious gift of the Holy Ghost will receive a certain amount of _____. This measure of _____ that everyone gets is the _____ of _____ referred to in _____.

Name the fruits of the Spirit?

_____ _____ _____

_____ _____ _____

_____ _____ _____

As we _____ and _____ in our walk with the Lord, we begin to produce His fruits.

In order to possess these _____, we have to _____ something. In order to use these _____, we have to _____ something. In order to _____ them, we have to _____ something.

What are you doing to possess, use and keep your fruits of the Spirit?

_____

_____

_____

_____

_____

_____

In order for our faith the remain alive, we must _____.

Works are different than an ordinance. An ordinance is _____.
_____.

List the works talked about in Matthew chapter 5 that will grow us in the Lord:

_____   _____

_____   _____

List the works talked about in Matthew chapter 5 that can lead us away from the Lord:

_____   _____

_____   _____

Evangelizing is the ultimate work of the Lord that will grow our fruit of faith. Who have you evangelized to in the past month?

_____

_____

_____

_____

_____

We must also recognize that our _____ are just one part of our _____ walk and they can either lead us to _____ or to _____.

In order for us to produce the fruits that we find in our Savior, we have to be:

_____   _____

_____   _____

Chapter Summation

After diving into the fruits of the Spirit and our works, what have you learned?

_____

_____

_____

_____

_____

_____

_____

_____

_____

Life Application

What do you plan to do differently going forward?

_____

_____

_____

_____

_____

_____

_____

_____

_____

Chapter 3 Review

- There is a difference between fruit of faith and gift of faith.
- Everyone who is filled with the Holy Ghost will receive the fruit of faith as well as the other fruits of the Spirit.
- In order for our fruit to remain alive, we must work.
- Our work, our job, being about our Father's business, is that of preaching the gospel of Jesus Christ. We are to be out there evangelizing to God's people.

- "The fruit of the Spirit is meant to be a list of qualities that will manifest themselves in our lives when we consciously decide to live according to God's word and be filled with the Holy Ghost."

Chapter 4

GIFT OF FAITH

Questions for You to Consider

Every good _____ and every perfect _____ is from above, and cometh down from the _____ of lights, with whom is no variableness, neither shadow of turning. James 1:17

Jesus is a _____ giver.

We give gifts nowadays to show appreciation, to celebrate an occasion, or even just to show good will. When was the last time that you gave a gift or received a gift? What was the reason behind the gift?

_____
_____
_____
_____
_____

All of us will receive sacrificial presents or gifts, but our Savior will give certain people certain specific gifts. Have you been given a spiritual endowment from the Holy Ghost? What are your spiritual gifts?

_____

_____

_____

_____

_____

_____

We receive this _____ _____ not for our own _____ but for the _____ of the _____.

Important factors to remember concerning spiritual gifts:

1) _____

2) _____

3) _____

4) _____

5) _____

God's _____ delivered through the _____ _____ are not for _____ and could not be _____ anyway.

What is the difference between the fruit of faith and the gift of faith?

_____

_____

_____

Chapter Summation

What have you learned pertaining to sacrificial gifts and spiritual endowments?

_____

_____

_____

_____

_____

_____

_____

_____

_____

Life Application

What do you plan to do differently going forward?

_____

_____

_____

_____

_____

_____

_____

_____

_____

_____

_____

Chapter 4 Review

- Every good and perfect gift comes from above from the Lord.
- Sacrificial gifts are not given to people based on their merit, but to anyone who has repented of their sin and desires them.
- Gifts are given for all sorts of reasons. But Christ loves us enough that if we simply ask for these gifts, He not only gives them to us, but He does it liberally and without faultfinding.
- Spiritual gifts are those gifts given by the Holy Spirit.
- Important factors to remember:
    - Every believer has been given spiritual gifts.
    - The gifts belong to God and are given for the believer to use for the glory of God.
    - We are expected to use the gifts that have been given to us.
    - We must accompany the use of our gifts with the right attitude.
    - We will have to give an account on judgment day for how we used our gifts.

> The difference between the fruit of faith and the gift of faith is that one is given to every Christian and it must be matured and cultivated: fruit. The other is a spiritual endowment that is meant to be used to edify the body of Christ and not everyone receives this: gift

Chapter 5

FAITH IS MORE THAN BELIEVING

Questions for You to Consider

_____ and _____ are very close in meaning but there is a definite _____.

When we _____ something, we take it at _____ _____.

People come to church initially because they _____ in God, but they receive _____ because they have _____ in God and His promises.

Faith is one-part _____ and one-part _____.

Belief is compared to faith like baking a cake. Can you think of another analogy to describe belief and faith?

_____

_____

_____

_____

What is your level of relationship with the Lord?

_____ Acquaintance _____ Feeling & Growth

_____ Confidence & Trust _____ Intimacy

Complete the staircase:

Chapter Summation

I thought that having faith and believing were synonymous. Did you have the same notion?

What can you do to shift from belief to faith?

_____

_____

_____

_____

_____

_____

_____

Life Application

What do you plan to do differently going forward?

_____

_____

_____

_____

_____

_____

_____

_____

_____

Chapter 5 Review

- Faith is distinct from human belief, but it does include it.
- Faith needs belief in order to be, but it is more than just belief because you have to add obedience to it.
- Climbing the stairs allows us to go from believing in Christ to having total faith in Him.

Chapter 6

FAITH THROUGH TESTIMONIES

Questions for You to Consider

Faith according to the Thomas Nelson New Open Bible is defined as "_____ in the _____ of another."

When we begin to _____ about the _____ of Christ, we are _____.

_____ comes from us _____ what Jesus has done for other people.

We have to _____ that sometimes when we are _____, it is not for us; it is for us to be a _____ for someone else.

When was the last testimony that you gave a testimony that glorified our Savior?

_____

_____

_____

_____

Can you think of a trial that you went through to be a testament to someone else? What was the trial and who was it truly for?

_____

_____

_____

_____

We can take whatever testimonies "laws or commandments" our God has given to us to the bank. Has every testimony you given to your children or received from your parents been scripture based?

_____

_____

_____

_____

Can you list the Ten Commandments from memory?

_____

_____

_____

_____

_____

_____

_____

_____

The written Word is our Lord and Savior's _____.

Chapter Summation

Our faith is increased by hearing others' testimonies. Others' faith is increased by hearing our testimony. Think of the last time you heard a powerful testimony and you knew that your faith shifted to a new level. Explain in detail the testimony and how your faith increased.

_____

_____

_____

_____

_____

_____

_____

_____

Life Application

What do you plan to do differently going forward?

_____
_____
_____
_____
_____
_____
_____
_____
_____
_____
_____

Chapter 6 Review

- Faith can be defined as "confidence in the testimony of another."
- Faith comes from us hearing what Jesus has done for other people, from hearing how He brought someone through a specific situation, how He delivered someone from an addiction, or how He healed someone's body from an illness.
- Some trials we go through are not strictly for us, but are for someone else as well.
- "Thy testimonies" is referring to God's laws or commandments.
- The Lord is daily downloading into our spirits His testimonies.

Chapter 7

JERI'S TESTIMONY

Questions for You to Consider

Jeri held on to her faith of her prophecies coming to pass for over six years. Is there something that you have asked the Lord for and have not yet it seen it come into fruition? Or a prophecy that has not come to pass yet?

_____

_____

_____

_____

_____

_____

_____

_____

_____

Is your faith still as strong today as it was when you first asked or heard? If not, why? If yes, what has helped it to remain so strong?

_____

Jeri was told that none of her prophecies would come to pass until she gave God a complete *yes* to His will. Is there something that you need to do before your prayers will be answered or your prophecy fulfilled?

Chapter Summation

Jeri began to walk out her faith. She went a picked out her wedding gown, and when it was marked down, she purchased it. Are you walking out your faith? If so, how? If not, why not?

_____

_____

_____

_____

_____

_____

_____

_____

Life Application

What do you plan to do differently going forward?

_____

_____

_____

_____

_____

_____

_____

_____

_____

Chapter 7 Review

- ➢ The Lord has given specific instructions in order for your prophecy to be fulfilled.

- ➢ God is not going to do His part until we do our part first.

- ➢ No matter how long you have to wait, keep the faith strong and walk out your faith.

Chapter 8

DANGEROUS D'S

Questions for You to Consider

What are the five areas the enemy tries to get us?

_____   _____

_____   _____

_____

The devil will not necessarily attack us _____ - _____ - _____ with open warfare, but rather, he will employ _____, _____ and _____ attacks.

Distractions are deployed to _____ you.

We are distracted: by _____, by _____, and by _____.

Have you ever been distracted by diversion? If yes, how were you able to redirect your focus back to the Lord?

_____

_____

_____

_____

_____

Distraction by divisions comes to us in five types: _____ _____, _____, _____, _____ and _____.

Have you ever been distracted by diverse doctrines? If yes, how were you able to overcome this distraction? .

_____

_____

_____

_____

_____

Have you ever been distracted by classification? If yes, how did you overcome this distraction?

_____

_____

_____

_____

Have you ever been distracted by personalities? If yes, how did you overcome this distraction?

_____

_____

_____

_____

_____

Have you ever been distracted by racism or sexism? If yes, how did you overcome this distraction?

_____

_____

_____

_____

_____

One of the biggest distraction devises used is the _____ of _____.

Have you ever been distracted by the seed of discord? If yes, how did you overcome this distraction?

_____

_____

_____

_____

_____

Be _____, be _____; because your adversary the _____, as a roaring lion, walketh about, seeking whom he may _____: 1 Peter 5:8

Chapter Summation

We all have faced distractions and they are going to continue to come as long as we have breath in our bodies and the devil is on his job. What are some things that you can do to divert those distractions?

_____

_____

_____

_____

_____

_____

_____

_____

_____

Life Application

What do you plan to do differently going forward?

_____

_____

Chapter 8 Review

- The enemy tries to get us by using doubt, discouragement, depression, despair and distractions.
- Distractions are deployed to destabilize you.
- We are distracted by diversion, by division, and by discord.
- Distractions by diversion are meant to divert your attention from Christ.
- Distractions by division are meant to ultimately divide the body of Christ. Not just from each other but also from Christ.
- Distractions by the seed of discord are the main tool of the enemy to divide God's people.
- In the beginning, distractions are not sin. But if not dealt with appropriately, can become sin.

Chapter 9

DOUBT

Questions for You to Consider

Distractions lead us to _____ God and His many _____ begin to seem _____ or out of _____.

Doubt translated from the Greek word _____ means "to waiver in opinion or doubt." This is phase one doubt.

Phase one doubt is a wanting of Christian faith. When was the last instance where you faced phase one doubt?

_____

_____

_____

_____

Neither Peter nor Thomas was able to overcome their phase one doubt without Jesus intervening on their behalf. How where you able to overcome your phase one doubt?

_____

With Faith Accompanying Workbook | 37

_____

_____

_____

_____

Doubt translated from the Greek word _____ means "to separate thoroughly to, from, or by implication oppose, to hesitate, to be partial, or doubt." This is phase two doubt.

Phase one doubt is manifested in our _____; however, phase two doubt is established in our _____.

Have you ever been faced with phase two doubt? What caused the doubt to shift from phase one to phase two? How did you combat the enemy?

_____

_____

_____

_____

What scripture can be used to speak against the doubt of paying tithes?

_____

What scripture can be used to speak against the doubt of not being able to pay bills?

What scripture can be used to speak against the doubt of not being able to put food on the table?

_____

_____

What scripture can be used to speak against the doubt of a loved one not being saved?

_____

_____

Create a cycle of "the more I pray with _____, the more the Lord will answer my _____. The more my prayers are _____, the greater my _____ will become. The greater my _____, the fewer cracks there are for _____."

Chapter Summation

We will all face doubt as long as the devil is still loose in the earth. What steps will you take to nip doubt in phase one?

_____

_____

_____

_____

_____

_____

Life Application

What do you plan to do differently going forward?

Chapter 9 Review

- Distractions lead us to doubt God and His many promises begin to seem small or out of reach.
- There are two phases to doubt. Phase one is an uncertainty of the mind, a wavering in opinion which comes from the Greek word *distazō*.

- Phase two doubt comes from the Greek word *diakrinō* which means "to separate thoroughly to, from, or by implication oppose, to hesitate, to be partial, or doubt." In phase two of doubt, we have chosen to thoroughly separate ourselves from, or completely oppose something that we once believed to be true.
- We all will face doubt, but it is our responsibility to be on guard to fight against it.
- Remedy for doubt.
    - Study the word of God.
    - Confess the doubt to the Lord.
    - Earnestly pray.

Chapter 10

UNBELIEF

Questions for You to Consider

_____ paves the way for _____.

The word _____ is used to depict two types of people in the bible. The first type comes from the Greek word _____ which means "faithlessness, disbelief (but a want of Christian _____), unfaithfulness (disobedience) – unbelief." The second type comes from the Greek word _____ which means "disbelief (_____ and _____) – disobedience, unbelief."

Have you ever had unbelief similar to that of the father of the demon possessed son? What incident brought about this unbelief?

_____

_____

_____

_____

Have you ever had to help someone else through this type of unbelief? How were you able to aid them?

_____

_____

_____

_____

_____

_____

The second type of _____ is exemplified by the _____ and scribes that would come to _____ Jesus as he taught and healed the people. Their _____ was _____ and a _____ of _____.

Have you ever had the pleasure of dealing with an atheist or someone who just would not change their way of thinking pertaining to the scriptures? How did your encounter play out?

_____

_____

_____

_____

Have you ever been broached with a subject that you felt confident enough to discuss but later felt inadequate on the matter? How did you rectify it?

_____

_____

_____

_____

_____

If _____ is _____ and disobedience is _____, then _____ is _____.

Chapter Summation

What areas of unbelief do you need converted to faith? Dig deep!

_____

_____

_____

_____

_____

_____

_____

_____

Life Application

What do you plan to do differently going forward?

_____

_____

_____

_____

_____

_____

_____

_____

_____

_____

Chapter 10 Review

- Doubt paves the way for unbelief.

- There are two types of unbelief.

  - *Apistia* which means "faithlessness, disbelief (but a want of Christian faith)"

    Apěithěia which means "disbelief (obstinate and rebellious)"

- Unbelief in any form is considered sin.

- We all have areas of unbelief that we need to convert to faith because unbelief will prevent us from seeing the mighty works of Christ.

- Steps to alter our unbelief into faith:

  - Repent and have true repentance for the unbelief.

  - Begin to read the word of God more, to memorize the word of God more, and to meditate on the word of God more.

  - Be obedient to the word of God.

    - If unbelief is disobedience, then obedience breeds belief.

Chapter 11

MY FEARS

Questions for You to Consider

For most of my life I have been afraid of bugs. What fears have you been facing for quite some time?

_____

_____

_____

_____

My fear of bugs was absolutely crippling at times. It made me late from picking up my daughter from school. Do your fears interfere with your life?

_____

_____

_____

_____

The Lord wanted to use me but was unable to as I also had a fear of public speaking. How is the Lord wanting to use but unable to because of your fears?

_____

_____

_____

_____

_____

I was eventually delivered of my fears in 2015. Have you been freed from your fears? If not, what's holding you back?

_____

_____

_____

_____

_____

Chapter Summation

After taking a deeper look into your fears, what have you learned about yourself? About fear?

_____

_____

_____

_____

Life Application

What do you plan to do differently going forward?

_____

_____

_____

_____

_____

_____

_____

Chapter 11 Review

> ➤ We are all going to have to face our fears one day.

> ➤ The Lord can't use you while you are allowing fear to have control.

- Once you are freed of your fear, then the Lord will truly begin to use you in your full capacity.

Chapter 12

FEAR BY SATAN

Questions for You to Consider

_____ is the first step towards _____ that could lead us to _____ if not properly addressed.

For _____ hath not given us the spirit of _____; but of _____, and of _____, and of a _____ _____. II Timothy 1:7

Fear is a very _____, _____ power.

Have you witnessed crippling fear in the life of someone else? Were you able to help them overcome their fear?

_____

_____

_____

_____

_____

_____ is the counterpoint of _____.

_____ and faith cannot _____. One will always _____ the other _____.

Think back to the last time you had faith for or about something and fear came in and canceled it out. Explain the situation.

_____

_____

_____

_____

_____

Fear is _____ natural to the _____ believer.

Where the _____ _____ reigns, fear has to _____.

Chapter Summation

It is impossible for fear and faith to dwell together in your heart. How will you equip yourself to fight against the spirit of fear?

_____

_____

_____

_____

_____

_____

Life Application

What do you plan to do differently going forward?

_____

_____

_____

_____

_____

_____

_____

_____

Chapter 12 Review

- ➢ We are not appropriately tackling fear.
- ➢ God did not give us the spirit of fear.
- ➢ Fear is destroying lives on a daily basis.
- ➢ Fear is the complete opposite of faith.

- Fear is a spiritual force that has been perverted and twisted by satan himself.
- Fear is a spirit sent by the devil himself in an attempt to drive away the fruit of faith which is a manifestation of the Holy Spirit abiding in our hearts.
- To completely annihilate and wipe out fear, we need love. Where the Holy Ghost reigns, fear has to flee.
- Once you have completely removed fear from you, DO NOT allow the devil to return to you with it.

Chapter 13

FEAR OF THE LORD

Questions for You to Consider

On the other side of the _____ coin is what can be called a _____ _____.

God is our _____ but He is also our _____ Lord and for that _____ alone we are to always have a _____ _____ of Christ.

When we _____ the Lord we will hate _____.

The Bible is full of examples of great men and women who feared the Lord. Describe someone in your life who fears the Lord.

_____

_____

_____

_____

_____

To fear the _____ is completely and utterly the _____ of the kind of fear the _____ attempts to bring to us.

Chapter Summation

"Who would not fear thee, O King of nations? for to thee doth it appertain: forasmuch as among all the wise men of the nations, and in all their kingdoms, there is none like unto thee," Jeremiah 10:7. I pose the same question to you, who would not fear the King of nations?

_____
_____
_____
_____
_____
_____
_____
_____
_____
_____

Life Application

What do you plan to do differently going forward?

_____
_____
_____
_____
_____

_____

_____

_____

_____

Chapter 13 Review

- When the scriptures state "the fear of the Lord," they are referring to a reverential fear.

- When we have a fear of the Lord, it is the beginning of wisdom.

- We cannot serve both God and the devil so we must either fear God, love Him, and fulfill His plans for us, or be a slave to the devil.

- We are to fear or reverence Christ and reject any fear that is dropped at our feet by our adversary.

- *"Now therefore fear the Lord, and serve him in sincerity and in truth: and put away the gods which your fathers served on the other side of the flood, and in Egypt; and serve ye the Lord. And if it seem evil unto you to serve the Lord, choose you this day whom ye will serve; whether the gods which your fathers served that were on the other side of the flood, or the gods of the Amorites, in whose land ye dwell: but as for me and my house, we will serve the Lord" Joshua 24:14-15.*

Chapter 14

WITH FAITH

Questions for You to Consider

_____ is the confident assurance in _____ _____ that the things we have _____ for are going to happen and are _____, even though we have not _____ _____ _____.

We have read about people in the Bible who were healed because of their faith. Do you know of anyone who was healed because of their faith in Christ Jesus?

_____

_____

_____

_____

How do you think Jesus would react if we asked something of Him and then activated our faith without doubting or having a backup plan?

_____

_____

_____

_____

_____

With faith we are justified. By our _____ that we have in _____ _____, we are now _____ to be guilt _____, or _____.

The just _____ live by _____.

With _____ we have access to God's _____.

What are the components to the Whole Armor of God? Why is the shield of faith so important?

_____

_____

_____

_____

We walk with _____ and not by _____.

_____ _____, our outlook is completely _____. It's like having on a pair of _____ that allows you to see the _____ instead of the _____.

If we pray with _____ asking for those things that are in _____ perfect will, we shall _____ them.

_____ is the only _____ to unlock the _____ of God.

Chapter Summation

We understand that it is impossible to please the Lord without faith. What will you do to eat, breath, and sleep faith?

_____

_____

_____

_____

_____

_____

_____

_____

_____

Life Application

What do you plan to do differently going forward?

_____

_____

_____

_____

Chapter 14 Review

- Faith is perceiving as real fact what is not yet revealed to the senses.

- Consider how pleased God is when we use our faith.

- We can read throughout the Bible what faith has done for so many people.

- With faith we are justified.

- Being considered just, we can't live without faith.

- The most important component of the whole armor of God is the shield of *faith* because the word informs us that our faith overcomes the world.

- We walk with faith and not by sight.

- In order for us to know the totality of God - His breadth, His length, His depth and His height, we have to operate in faith.

Chapter 15

TIFFANY'S TESTIMONY

Questions for You to Consider

Tiffany prayed continuously to hear from the Lord concerning her working at SLU. She didn't move, but instead stayed the course until she heard from the Lord. Is this your testimony as well? Have you stayed put until you heard from the Lord on your next move?

_____

_____

_____

_____

When Tiffany finally did hear from the Lord, she didn't move punctually. Can this be said about you or do you move immediately when you hear God's voice?

_____

_____

_____

_____

Once Tiffany had a clear understanding of what she was to do, she walked off her job and took a leap of faith. Have you ever taken a drastic leap of faith? What was the outcome?

_____

_____

_____

_____

Despite the naysayers in Tiffany's life, she held on to her faith and was rewarded with the perfect job right out of nursing school. Do you listen to the naysayers in your life or do you keep the faith?

_____

_____

_____

_____

Tiffany's faith walk didn't end upon receiving the perfect job. She continued to walk out her faith as she accepted the prophecy and returned to school. How will you continue to walk out your faith as you pass each faith test?

_____

_____

Chapter Summation

Tiffany has been a testament to "crazy faith". What is your definition of "crazy faith" and are you willing to abide in it?

Life Application

What do you plan to do differently going forward?

_____

_____

_____

_____

_____

_____

_____

_____

Chapter 15 Review

- The Lord will always be there with you as you walk out your faith.
- As you begin to walk with faith, Jesus will open doors for you that no man can close.
- No matter how far-fetched it seems, be obedient to the Lord and watch Him move on your behalf.
- Sometimes you must take a leap of faith. Just remember that "fear looks, but faith jumps."

Book Summation

Questions for You to Consider

This book breaks down the aspects of faith and its counterparts. What is the biggest takeaway for you and why?

_____
_____
_____
_____
_____
_____
_____

Life Application

What do you plan to do differently going forward?

_____
_____
_____
_____
_____

What has reading and studying this book meant to you?

NOTES

NOTES

Made in the USA
Columbia, SC
05 March 2022